Around Alto.
In Former Days

A Hampshire Man Remembers

Written and illustrated by

James G. Adams

© James G Adams Articles and illustrations
© Robert Adams 2004 editorial
matter and introduction

All rights reserved. No reproduction, copy or transmission of this publication may be made without written permission.

ISBN No. 1-84503-013-3

A catalogue record for this book is available from the British Library

The illustrations on the front and back covers of this book are by James G. Adams.

First published in 2004 by

**Bitterne Books
PO Box 606
Hull HU5 3WW**

Acknowledgements

Acknowledgements are due for the following individual items published by *The Alton Gazette* and reproduced by kind permission of the editor:
Fun of the Alton fair originally printed 8 May 1996
Alton Railways on Film originally printed 19 June 1996, drawn on in *Alton's Trains of Long Ago*
Yesterday's Alton originally published 24 April 1996, drawn on in *The Alton I remember*

Acknowledgements are due for the following individual items originally published in *Hampshire, The County Magazine* reproduced (in edited versions) here, by kind permission of the editor:
The Alton I remember originally printed in January 1991 p. 27
A Holybourne Choirboy's Memory originally printed January 1990 pp. 43-4
Alton's Trains of Long Ago, originally printed in June 1989 pp. 34, 36
The Black Dog of Ashdell, originally printed in February 1993 pp. 59, 61, drawn on in chapter 4
Hop Picking originally printed in *Hampshire* November 1989 pp. 35-6
The School at Lane End originally printed in April 1992 pp. 35-6
The Old Malt House, Privett originally printed in Sept 1988 p. 47
Deflation at the Treloar Hospital originally published August 1986 p. 55

Christmas at Treloars, originally printed in December 1992 p. 50

Thanks are due to Walter Brown, Jim's brother in law, for reading through a draft of chapter 9 for Jim and his help to Jim in supplying much of the detail concerning Lane End school, featured in chapter 9.

Other titles by the author:

Growing up through the Great War
A Sussex Witch and other Stories
Ashcote: Tales from a
Hampshire Village
Tales from Old Wessex
Snapshots of Bygone Days

In memory of

James G. Adams 1908 to 1997

and

Winifred M. Adams 1917 to 1979

Contents

Introduction
    Memories - Poem
1 Winchester
    Water Meadows - Poem
2 Colden Common
    Holybourne Church Pond - Poem
3 A Holybourne Choirboy's Memory
    The Village Church - Poem
    A Holybourne Lane - Poem
4 The Alton I Remember
5 Fun of the Alton Fair
6 Alton's Trains of Long Ago
7 Hop Picking
8 The Old Malt House at Privett
9 The School at Lane End
10 Deflation at the Treloar Hospital
11 Christmas at Treloars
    Passing Time - Poem

Introduction

James George Adams was born on 13 December 1908. He spent his early years in Winchester, moving to West Sussex and back again to Hampshire during the Great War. He died 6 May 1997. His parents lived in Hampshire. In spirit he was a Hampshire man. 'Jim', as he was known to many, lived in Hampshire nearly all his adult working life. He married Winifred Mary Adams (née Brown) in 1938 and she died on 20 April 1979. There were three children, Pat, who died at the age of 50 in 1989, and Robert and Godfrey, now living in the north of England.

This collection takes us back to the early years of the twentieth century, and records Jim's moves from Winchester to Colden Common, Holybourne and Alton. Chapter 7 records how Jim's sister Sabina, known as 'Bine', joined the widespread local custom of hop picking, in the harvesting season. Chapter 9 records how in the 1920s and 30s, Jim met, courted and married Win. The last two chapters refer to the five years from 1928 when he worked in the Lord Mayor Treloar hospital, Alton.

This collection is drawn partly from Jim's unpublished writing and partly from many articles he wrote, published in the magazine *Hampshire* and in the *Alton Gazette*. We are grateful to the editors of these publications for permission to reproduce these articles here, several in much edited form.

Robert and Godfrey Adams

Memories

The fields of grass - a sea - which ripples in the breeze,
And in the spinney leaves are trembling on the trees,
It's but a mild air movement here and everywhere,
Breathes gently on the countryside so fresh and fair.

It takes me to the scene I knew so long ago,
In which are figured faces which once I used to know;
Those self-same ripples waved the grass upon the hill
Where picnics of those days are gone, but harebells grow there still.

1 Winchester

I spent the first seven years of my life in Winchester. Most weeks, my mother took my sister and me to visit my aunt Lily and buy eggs from her. Aunt lived at 13 Bridge Street from the time she married uncle Arthur Eyles, later killed at the Dardanelles, until she died in an old people's home aged 99.

I had five young cousins - Jim, May, Daisy, Hilda and Georgie the toddler - and it was always fun to meet them. Jim was the eldest, several years older than me.

We saved our food scraps for aunt Lily's hens and fed them when we arrived. Jim used to fish in the weir. He kept his fishy captives in a brick outhouse - minnows, redbreasts, sticklebacks and newts, which I found a most interesting collection at that age.

One Christmas Eve, mother took us to aunt Lily's. We arrived in the evening and our cousins were ready for bed, each with a stocking ready to hang up.

'Are you going to hang up your stocking?' Jim asked me.

I told him I was and said what I hoped Father Christmas would bring me.

'There's no Father Christmas,' Jim jibed. 'It's your mum and dad who put the things in your stockings.'

This display of ignorance shattered me. I argued, of course, helped by Daisy, Hilda and my sister, who were all on my side. When we left, I told my mother what a lot of rubbish Jim had spoken. I had the feeling mother agreed with me as she said something like

'You mustn't always take notice of what some people say.'

To some extent Jim redeemed himself in my eyes when he joined the Royal Navy. Before joining up, he came to stay with us for several weeks. One day he had a good idea.

'We'll make a kite,' he announced.

We combed hedges and spinneys looking for straight hazel sticks, one large one from top to bottom and a shorter cross spar. We tied the sticks with twine and glued light paper onto it. We attached a tail and took our kite to a nearby field.

At first our kite nose-dived and crashed, but after repairing it with tougher brown paper, and lengthening the tail, we thought we had solved its problems. No matter what we did to that kite that day, it didn't seem to want to fly.

After a couple of weeks, Jim started in the Royal Navy. After the Navy he was to start a builder's business which he ran until the 1990s, when he died of a heart attack.

Jim left me the kite which, I should add, reached from the ground up to above my shoulders. He also left me lots of instructions on what to do to make it fly.

Well, I have to admit, I thought it was a jolly good-looking kite. I used to sit up in bed and look at it propped against my bedroom wall. Unfortunately, it never flew.

Water Meadows

The water meadows lush and green,
To me they were the best I'd seen.
But then, at six years old I know
I'd still a long, long way to go.

In years to come there would be more
Such meadows to be seen, I'm sure,
But how could I then aware be
What future things I'd live to see?

I only knew what I saw then
And just of past and present ken.
The future never concerned me
'Twas only then that I could see.

I saw the river running past
The kingcups, it was rushing fast.
Yellow flags, bullrushes, too
Were on the banks which it flowed through.

At times I'd go with jar and net
To see what minnows I could get,
But like all anglers, I must say
The best ones always got away.

When I went home, which was not far
'Twas tadpoles only in my jar.
The captives were not of my quest,

I'd come back home with second best.

This, I accepted, was life's rule;
To argue, I would be a fool.
You cannot always win an ace,
Sometimes you're doomed to second place.

Strive for the top - of course you must,
Rememb'ring life is never just.
Do your best, and if you've tried,
That's good, be satisfied.

2 Colden Common

Esther Long was my great aunt, dead now for many years. She lived at 1 Diamond Villas, Colden Common near Winchester, with her parents and then with my grandmother. Great aunt Esther was badly disabled from childhood polio which had twisted her feet and body so she could only hobble a few yards at a time, with the help of a stick. She never left the house, except in an old-fashioned 3-wheeled wickerwork bathchair.

In those days, pensions were not paid before 70 and a sick or disabled person relied on the family for support. Great aunt Esther supported herself through her talent for making artificial silk flowers which looked so natural people thought they were real. It was the age when ladies still wore hats lavishly adorned with sprays of artificial flowers.

Ladies from the neighbourhood, such as Mrs Mordaunt Shipley of Twyford Moors, Miss Auten of 'The Glen', would make afternoon calls to choose selections from her stock or to leave orders. Some ladies brought silk and other materials in the shades they wanted using.

On one occasion, I remember a caller, apparently very deaf, producing a large silver ear trumpet from her fur muff where it was hidden.

This ear trumpet interested me so much, once or twice I peeped into the room where the artificial flower transactions were going on. I saw great aunt Esther trying to make herself understood as she spoke as loudly as she could into the ear trumpet. Many times I wished I could have the opportunity of answering the door to this lady's knock, for the chance to say something into the ear trumpet.

My great grandmother herself was very deaf. To see these two deaf women, one with an ear trumpet, trying to make each other understand, was somewhat comical. Maybe I was unkind in this, but that would not necessarily be how it would appear to a nine year-old boy.

Holybourne Church Pond

Beside the hallowed churchyard lies a pool so calm and deep,
Whilst all around the guardian trees their watchful vigil keep;
The only sound is of the birds and footsteps on the way -
The sexton comes the bell to toll to sound the close of day.

Each evening time farm horses come to drink the water cool.
They seem to find much pleasure as they walk out in the pool;
A small boy there is hopeful armed with fishing net and jar.
He'll be satisfied with minnows or whatever fish there are.

From a small islet in the pool some scraggy bushes grow;
A little moorhen and her mate towards this islet go.
The pond, it has some visitors - ducks from the nearby farm.
But these are only here to feed and won't do moorhens harm.

The outlet from the pond is through a metal small-barred trap.

From this cascade the water falls with loud resounding slap;
'Tis carried on through wild cress clumps by swift stream to the Wey
And thence it flows through field and town to the sea far away.

3 A Holybourne Choirboy's Memory

1920 seems, and really is a lifetime away, and it was at the end of that year that I reached my twelfth birthday. It was the year when my family moved to the quiet village of Holybourne, a little village about two miles from the centre of the Hampshire town of Alton. I was used to the country and, after about three years in Southsea, it suited me well to be back in a village community again. There were many things in Southsea not available in villages: large shops, places of entertainment and the beach, though this was probably used far less often by Southsea people than by holiday makers. I had left these behind and instead spent my days in narrow leafy lanes, with fields and hop gardens beyond the hedges.

How different things seemed to me after living in Portsmouth for several years and enduring the wartime rationing. My father was away in the army and I remember sometimes the egg ration for the week for mother, sister and me was one egg, and how this had been boiled or fried and cut in half for my sister and me. Here in the village many folk kept hens and eggs were easy to buy.

A big change for sister and me were the school holidays which, instead of beginning in July and ending the latter part of August, began in August and ran on to the end of September. This was due to the fact that this was a hop-growing area. Not only did the farmers need to have pickers when the hops were ripe in September, the working folk looked to 'hopping' for a bit of extra cash to help the family through the early stages of winter.

At Holybourne, there were hop gardens belonging to Messengers, Twitchens and Complins, with some others in and around Alton and in nearby villages. I think many of the hop gardens have now disappeared. The hop-picking brought a number of gypsies into the area as there were not enough local folk to cover the job.

On Saturdays, the gypsies would flood into Alton in horse-drawn carts of all descriptions. The public houses did a good trade and when the drinking had finished, arguments broke out between the gypsy families. It was fortunate the police knew how to deal with these situations, returning the contestants to their carts and sending them on their way.

The traffic using the main road through the village was light, though over years it built up enormously. Later, the build-up was halted when the Alton by-pass blocked the through-road at Cuckoo's Corner. Chawton, on the other side of Alton, enjoyed a similar relief when its through road was cut off.

There was a two-mile walk to Alton for shopping because there were no buses when we came to Holybourne. There were two excellent shops, though, one owned by Mr. Mark Piggott, located beside the White Hart hotel, the other owned by Mr. Purkess. A few elderly ladies used a donkey and trap provided by Mrs. Mercy Hall who kept the sweet shop at the Alton end of the village, for lifts to town. The donkey, Peggy, was somewhat unpredictable and often cantankerous. She could sometimes only be persuaded to continue the journey after being bribed with sweets or chocolate.

The first time I went with my family to the church, we had a warm welcome. I revisited the church several times fifty years later and understood this feeling. Mellow with age, the little church stands in a green churchyard with silent trees and lichen-covered tombstones marking final resting places of villagers long dead. The plain, peaceful interior of the church, whose walls have absorbed the prayers and praise of many generations, brings home to one the reason for being there. Apart from the distant sound of water falling gently from the pond into the stream, silence is all around. There is seldom interference from road traffic noise from the lanes which bound two sides of the churchyard. On another side is a field and the banks of Church Pond form the remaining boundary. Here in this churchyard, are the springs which rise to fill the pond and set the stream The Bourne on its way to join a tributary of the River Wey in meadows a mile or so away. This stream gives the village its name of Holybourne.

The village school I attended was a church school and the vicar came once a week to give a scripture lesson. No doubt the boys he saw there were a prime source from which choirboys could be selected. Reverent Peacock, the vicar in those days, saw me at school soon after we came to the village, together with two of my friends, Arthur and Eddie Martin, who had also been in the village a week or two. He immediately saw our parents to ascertain whether they would agree to our being enrolled as choirboys.

I already had some choir training when we lived in Southsea, so singing a solo test piece to the organist and choirmaster did not perturb me. It would have been more comfortable, however, had I not looked into the mirror above the organist to see other choirboys giggling at me. That mirror was important as it enabled the organist to see whether any boy was misbehaving during services. To the same end, Major Pole, one of the churchwardens, sat in the congregation in a place from which he could keep an eye on the choir.

When I joined the choir, the organist and choirmaster was a Mr. Young, followed later by M. Robert Hayward who kept a wool and fancy-goods shop in Alton. Our head choirboy was 'Ginger' Simpson. The names of some of the other choirboys come to mind: Will Warner, Bert Trimmer, Reg Gates, Jerry Simpson, Fred Oakley, the two Martins, Frank and 'Bunny' Binfield. Sadly for all of us, Frank Binfield died while still a choirboy. Mr. Trimmer (Bert's father) and a Mr. Faithful were the choir men, and Miss Mabel Piggott and Miss Faithful were the ladies in the choir.

Acceptance into the choir would not have been right without some sort of initiation ceremony by existing choirboys. Following our first Friday practice, the Martins and I were hustled to the edge of the pond to be semi-ducked. Whether it was just the head which went in the water or more of the body, depended on how much the victim struggled. I must have been quite a handful, as it was my feet and not my head that actually dipped into the water.

In those days, the bellows for the organ had to be manually operated. Our organ blower was Bill Binfield, an older brother of Frank and Bunny. He was probably in his early twenties, quite good-natured but maybe somewhat slow. As soon as Bill knew the sermon had started, he would go out from the vestry where perhaps a pal would be waiting and they would chat and smoke a cigarette or two. The bellows did not hold up to full pressure and, as soon as the blower stopped pumping, one would see the pressure indicator blob in the vestry start to fall. Another fault was, if Bill became too energetic before the sermon and continued to pump after the organist stopped playing, a loud squeak was emitted from one of the high notes, audible all over the church.

Soon after I joined the choir, the organist fell ill and for several weeks the vicar's wife officiated as organist. On one of these Sunday mornings, the sermon was shorter than usual and when Mrs. Peacock attempted to play the introduction to the hymn there was no wind at all in the bellows. She rattled the keys loudly several times to no avail. Then, in desperation, she called out loudly over the silence of the waiting congregation, 'Blow up, Binfield. Blow up.'

But there was no Binfield to blow up and Ginger Simpson left the choir to take over the organ blower's duties until he returned. Shortly afterwards, Bill returned to the vestry. He had gone for a walk whilst the sermon was preached and forgotten the time.

Although it may sound silly today, it was not out of the way in those days for choirboys to receive a little pay. We were paid once a quarter at the rate of twopence for Sunday services, provided we attended both matins and evensong. We received nothing for that day if we missed a service. For children's services we received no pay, as we were supposed to be at Sunday school in any case.

One thing choirboys did appreciate: we were allowed out of school on such days, as we were required for special or Saints' Day services. These ranked for extra pay which I think was about a penny. On these days, we must have looked a pretty scruffy crowd of boys presenting itself at the vestry door. Football, marbles or some such messy game might have been played before school and during break, so we would be with muddy boots, dirty knees - we all wore shorts in those days - not very clean hands and hair anything but tidy. Hair would be pulled to a more or less tidy state. None of us had the luxury of possessing a comb. Cassocks successfully covered up dirty knees and boots, grubby hands were clasped together in front of our surplices in a submissive sort of way as we processed round the church pews from vestry to choir stalls, all of us probably looking the innocent little cherubs which we certainly were not.

Nowadays, the long procession around the central block of pews is not done. We used to come out of the vestry along the aisle leading to the secondary entrance door, along the back of the church and up the central aisle to the stalls. Now some of the front pews of the central block have been removed, there is a short-cut from vestry to choir stalls.

The pews near the secondary entrance were reserved more or less on Sunday mornings for Sunday school children. Mr. Mark Piggott from one of the village shops always sat there and he saw the Sunday school children behaved themselves.

I think there was little doubt the choirboys enjoyed the services in the main, except perhaps on those Sunday mornings when we had to kneel for a long time while the Litany was sung. We all seemed to find this a boring part of the service.

The choirboys were required to attend church for funeral services, if someone of importance died and also for wedding ceremonies. I think we sometimes received as much as threepence for such an attendance.

In previous years, there was always some annual function for the choir, an outing or some such event, but there was not one while I was in the choir. The vicar who followed Rev. Peacock was Rev. Beardall and he looked after the choirboys very well. He would sometimes take us all to the Alton cinema to see a cowboy film. He would arrange picnics for us in his orchard, with the maids from the vicarage handing us round all kinds of cakes and sandwiches. There were occasions when we were invited to come to the vicarage orchard to collect and take home paper bags filled with whatever fruit was available.

Rev. Beardall eventually left Holybourne for another parish and it was there he passed away.

Well, I am still here, though very much older. I wonder what happened to those other boys who were in the choir with me in 1921. Some may have been in the Forces during the war, never to return. Others will have left the village for a number of reasons: work took them away; families moved. Any who are left, no doubt like myself, will have memories of the days when we were choirboys together at Holybourne and perhaps they still sing, wherever they may be.

Church of The Holy Rood
Holybourne.

The Village Church

This fine old church for many years
A sanctuary has been;
Events of happiness and tears,
Its old stone walls have seen.

The clock it gives us all the time,
At this it never fails.
Each hour it tells with strike and chime,
Its ardour never pales.

Each Sunday from the tower goes out
The call to folk for prayer,
And this is met by those devout,
Who come and worship there.

A wedding - the bells ring for joy -
A happy sound to hear;
At Christmas for a Baby Boy
Then later, for New Year.

A pity bells aren't always glad.
A passing? Sound the knell;
Which means that many may be sad,
But do not blame the bell.

A Holybourne Lane

It used to be called Butcher's Lane, but that was years ago.
Perhaps today 'tis called the same, though that I do not know.
I remember its fine hedges which ran along each side
And many little animals and birds would in them hide.

Of many kinds of bush and tree those hedgerows did comprise.
Blackberries, sloes and rose hips the locals thought a prize,
For these in great abundance grew for picking when quite ripe,
And on the hazel branches there the brown nuts were my type.

Rank grass and many other plants beside the hedgerows grew
And hiding there was where we found sweet violets white and blue.
To find them there among the growth one's back had to be bent,
But having picked a posy one had beauty and a scent.

Alas, these days some scenes have changed and many hedgerows gone;

Removed and lost forever - sad sight to look upon.
Not only have we lost the joy but wild creatures lost their home;
This is the way to make our land an empty barren zone.

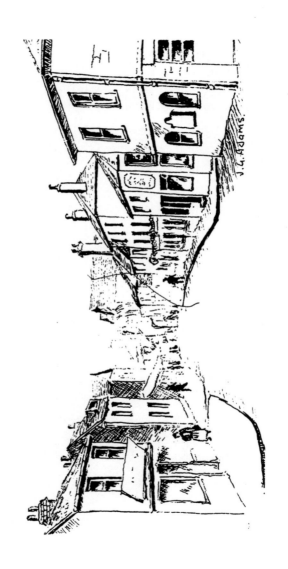

4 The Alton I Remember

When we moved to 1 Albert Road in the early 1920s, the Territorial Army drill hall existed. It stood on one corner of Butts Road and Albert Road and extended down as far as the fence which ran beside our house. Houses are now built where the drill hall used to be. In those days, Albert Road was a *cul de sac* with the Roman Catholic Church and priest's house at the end, hard by the five-barred field gate and stile leading to Mr Batten's hop garden. The hop garden disappeared some years ago and a housing estate has been built on the land.

In the early 1920s, I started my first job with Mr E A Walters, a contractor and coal merchant of Ackender Road, who was opening a small order office in Normandy Street. I was employed to run it and take enquiries for haulage work, removals and orders for coal. My hours were from 8 am. To 6 pm. However, soon after the office started running, there was a change to my working hours. Many of the carters and drivers were unable to deal with time-sheets and it was arranged that I go to the yard at 6.30 am. every morning to see the men before they left the yard for whatever work they had to do, and write up the time-sheets for the work they had done the day before. This took me a full hour and then I went home for a quick breakfast before walking to Normandy Street to open the office at 8 o'clock.

I have a keen memory of the hop garden in those days, as it afforded me a somewhat muddy and sticky short cut between Albert Road and Ackender Road.

In those days, the Alton Gasworks was in operation and my trek through the hop garden took me along by the back hedge of the gasworks meadow (now Borovere Gardens). It was in this meadow that local football teams played. The Alton Wednesdays used the field during the week and the Alton Federation on Saturday.

In the early 1920s, Alton was a small, pleasant town with a large market for cattle, sheep, pigs, poultry and dairy produce, as well as miscellaneous items, held every Tuesday in and adjoining the market square. Around the town was some delightful countryside with beautiful walks and attractive villages, most of which, fortunately, remain untouched.

Everything changes, ways of life as well as places, and Alton itself has not escaped. The population in the early 1920s was about 6,000. But families moving in from the Greater London area following wartime bombing created a rise in the population. Also the town became a commuter area. Many of the old places I knew either have changed beyond recognition or have disappeared.

There was always something to do in the town in those days. For those who liked to listen to, or join in, musical activities, there was the Alton Town Band, under the direction of Mr. Henry Lugg. The Salvation Army also had a very good band conducted by Mr.

John Knight. There were three dance bands with good instrumentalists, there was a small philharmonic orchestra, as well as the orchestra which played for the Gilbert and Sullivan operas produced every year.

The Alton Dramatic Society was go-ahead and was responsible for some well-known plays. Also, for theatre goers, some repertory companies put on shows for several years at the Foresters' Hall. The cinema flourished, with different programmes for the first three days and the second three days of the week. One must not overlook the Alton Debating Society, which met fortnightly and had an enthusiastic following. Exhibitions were held from time to time in the Assembly Rooms. But perhaps the event which evoked most local interest was the Annual Chrysanthemum Show, which gave Alton gardeners the chance to show their best flowers, fruit and vegetables. For the younger set, dances were arranged each week, by one or other of the local dance bands.

Of the many changes which have taken place in the town, I wonder how many people realise Whitedown Estate was once the football ground for Courage's Brewery, bounded by Chawton Park Road, Whitedown Lane, the Basingstoke Railway and Bill Vince's little farm. The players' pavilion backed onto the Treloar Hospital railway siding.

Facing the Butts, close by the French Horn public house, were some old thatched cottages, now modernised and tiled. In one of these lived Mr. Christmas, who had a wood yard, and his disabled son Jake. They used to deliver fire logs by wheelbarrow to householders at sixpence a bushel.

An old German field gun from the 1914-18 war stood where the telephone kiosk now stands, opposite Albert Road.

In Mount Pleasant Road, opposite Barham's smithy, was a small cottage occupied by a short, tubby couple: Dick Wells, who worked for Mr. Orchard the saddler in Turk Street, and his sister. One would see this elderly lady, wearing a rough tweed coat with a cord round the middle, and a black felt hat, pushing a two-wheeled truck made from a packing case and pram wheels. She would be particularly busy on market days, or when there was an auction sale in the Market Square saleroom. She would charge a few coppers to shift items for purchasers.

Two more well-known local characters were poachers, the very lanky Liberty Wells and his father Sid. They came up before the Bench with great regularity.

Messrs Throwers' coach building works, D. J. Kemp's builders yard, Mr. Hayden's grocery shop, and the Wesleyan church, have all gone and a supermarket occupies these sites. The Wesleyan church had a Wayside Pulpit board carrying a new text each week. One day when I passed, the text was 'Drink is your worst enemy.' Unfortunately, that same week the Congregational Church opposite the cinema at the far end of town, had as its Wayside Pulpit message 'Make your worst enemy your friend.'

Mr. Gales had a large butcher's shop a little way from here. Shops in those days opened until eight or eight-thirty at night. His rotund figure would be seen late on Saturday evening, offering unsold joints of meat for a fraction of the normal price. A shilling or eighteen pence (five pence or seven and a half pence) would buy a joint of beef weighing three or four pounds.

On the opposite side of the road, the old lunatic asylum (Westbrook House) is now the local authority's offices and fire station. The grounds of the house are now public gardens and a car park. At one time, the fire station had been at Cut Pond. Before moving to its present site, it was in a part of the Council building in the Market Square. The Market Square was the venue for the two annual fairs in the early 1920s, before these moved to the Butts.

Opposite Turk Street used to be Timothy White's and Woolworth's, and next door was the greengrocery shop belonging to Mr. Herbert Pavey. I remember him telling me a lady came to him on a Saturday evening and said 'How much are your tomatoes, Mr. Pavey?'

'Tenpence a pound, lady,' he told her.

'Oh dear,' she said. 'That's a lot. At the Home and Colonial Stores opposite, they're only ninepence.'

'Then that's where you should buy them lady.'

'But they haven't any left,' she complained.

'Well lady, when I've sold out, mine will be eightpence a pound,' he told her.

Turk Street led to Crowley's and Courage's breweries and on the corner of the street was the Royal Oak Hotel (now the offices of estate agents). For a year or two, this public house was visited by an old soldier who lived out Wilsom way. He would come to town via Station Road and Normandy Street, followed by his pet goose. At that time of the evening, they were sedate and steady. But by the end of the evening things were different. They would both stagger towards home, with the goose, who apparently enjoyed a drink, flapping out first one wing then the other in order to keep on a more or less even keel.

It is a pity to see so many of the old shops have gone. The shop of Mr. B. F. Johnson on the corner of High Street and Market was a high-class draper. On the opposite corner was a baker and confectioner's shop run by Mr. Piper who, it was held, made the best dough cakes anywhere. Chesterfield's ladies and gent's outfitters was another large shop, now gone, with its place taken by banks. Almost next door was Kerridge's garage. It was this garage that put the first bus on the road for the district. True, it was a rather strange looking affair, box-like with an abundance of glass, which earned it the name of the 'Alton Greenhouse'. But it did move people around. It was taken over by Mr. Clifford of Chawton, who soon put a smarter vehicle on the road: the Ruby Queen.

Where the Co-op and several other shops later stood was the big house where Mr. Goodwyn Hall lived. His brother, Gerald, lived at Anstey Manor. At the back of the house were some fine grounds and a deer park, now the site of 'Harp' lager brewery.

Radio and television shops now are well represented. In those days, we spoke of 'wireless'. For the wireless fan, there was just one shop in Alton where sets or parts could be bought. First, it was in Lenten Street, later it moved to Normandy Street. Mr. Meadows ran this shop, in which one could buy coils, transformers, condensers, valves and so on, and, of course, for crystal sets, crystals and cats whiskers. Most of us were at the crystal set stage in those days, so when we needed some accessory it was natural for us to visit 'Whiskers' Meadows.

The town was quiet in those days as far as traffic was concerned. A horse bus used to stand outside the station to transport those passengers from the train. There were milk floats for the dairymen who used to call at the houses, ladling milk for customers, from a lidded bucket, using a half-pint or a pint measure.

A bigger float was used by Mr. Rapkins, the slaughterhouse man, and a similar vehicle collected parcels for the Treloar Hospital, from the station. One rather grand equipage was a coach driven by a liveried coachman. He had a cockaded top hat and fur tie and conveyed Mrs. Wickham of Wyck into town. On a warm night, everyone thought the coachman would have felt more comfortable if he could have dispensed with the fur draped around his neck.

One other character I recall was Dr. Leslie. All doctors nowadays make their house-calls by car. Dr. Leslie did not have a car. He was best remembered as going on horseback to visit his patients. He would be seen shouting at the top of his voice outside a patient's house, till someone came to the door. From his position astride the horse, he would ask the condition of the patient, bark out some instructions, perhaps give a prescription and call out 'Take two at night and one in the morning.' It was not strange that he was known as 'Two at night and one in the morning.'

Since the 1930s, when I have visited Alton I have seen many changes and have wondered whether the long flight of rough steps from Ashdell to part of Windmill Hill still exists. I never counted the steps, though they were referred to locally as 'the hundred steps'. As I walked along Ashdell Road I could glimpse the small deer park behind the house where Mr. Goodwin Hall lived.

On several occasions, walking along Ashdell, I became aware of a large black dog loping along in front of us. The first time this happened, I was taking a walk with two pals, George Bryant and Bill Hay. We never knew where the dog came from. He was just there, running ahead and then, just as suddenly, he had gone. The first time we took no notice, as there were often dogs taking themselves for a walk. But when we saw it on at least two more occasions, we thought it strange indeed. Though we tried to see where the dog had come from and gone, we never succeeded.

Recently, I was reading the book *An Ordinary Working Man's Life Story* by Joseph Cox, which referred to the black dog in Ashdell Road. I knew Joseph, as he lived near my parents and he and his wife knew my sister with whom they ran Old Tyme Dances in the town. He wrote the book when ending his days in the Alton hospital.

Joseph Cox was born in Ashdell Lodge in 1877. He explains in the book how the large Ashdell estate was developed by Mr. Fred Crowley the brewer and extended from Windmill Hill to Wilsom. Apparently, a Spanish man came from Gibraltar and build a large house he called 'Gibraltar', the grounds of which ran down to the River Wey. The Spaniard had a beautiful daughter with a black dog she loved. The girl's father forbade her to marry her sweetheart and one day she went missing. Afterwards, the dog was always running round searching for his mistress, especially at evening time. Joseph says he saw the dog in later years, loping along Ashdell and thought how strange it was when the animal suddenly vanished. He says once when his parents were living in the house as caretakers while Fred Crowley had taken it over and was away on honeymoon, sometimes during the night they would hear a door slam, followed by the sound of a dog panting and pattering up and down the stairs. Although Joseph's father got up and searched, he could never see anything of the dog.

I am sure if I was still living in Alton, I would have pursued this intriguing story.

5 Fun of the Alton Fair

Until the early 1920s, Alton's Michaelmas Fair was held in the Market Square. Of course, there were not as many sideshows as now make up the fair which is held on the Butts but, thinking back, it was surprising what amusements were packed into the Market Square.

Near Adlam's Bakery was the tall 'Try Your Strength' column with its bell at the top. Along by the wall of the central building, which was the old Council Offices, the coconut shy was fitted up. A line of swing boats was accommodated along by the rails to which cattle were tethered on market days. Every fair has its roundabout with galloping horses and this had pride of place in roughly the centre of the square

Surprisingly, hoop-la stalls, darts, ringboards and a shooting gallery were packed in somewhere and also there was a stall where brandy snaps and other fairground sweetmeats were sold.

Standing in the corner near the shed where Mr A J Martin held his auction sales, was the steam engine in all its glory, providing the power necessary to keep everything running. There is always a strong smell of oil from a steam engine and in the rather enclosed situation the smell was more noticeable, though probably not unpleasant.

Crowds of folk, not just those who lived in the town, but those from villages around, all gathered to enjoy the 'Fun of the Fair'. There is no doubt the crowd was dense, and it would perhaps seem impossible today to cram so much and so many persons into such a small space.

Eventually, the Council stopped the Market Square being used for this purpose and changed the venue to the Butts. Maybe this is better all round, but there was something which made the earlier fairs perhaps just a little more 'olde worlde' - or maybe that is just my private opinion.

6 Alton's Trains of Long Ago

I remember, and I am sure there will be many folk who will remember with nostalgia, the time when Alton station was the centre of quite a busy junction.

A service to London had existed for some years when the line connecting Alton to Winchester began in 1861. For about the first four years of its life it was known as the Alresford and Winchester Railway Company, after which it took on the name of the Mid-Hants Railway and was operated by the old London and South Western Railway. For people using the line from stations along its seventeen miles stretch it was now easy to catch connections for London from either Alton or Winchester.

Also operating from Alton was the Meon Valley line, which served passengers using the stations in the direction of Portsmouth. There was also the branch line to Basingstoke, which had a number of 'halts' along its ten mile length.

The line to Basingstoke had once been operated until the 1914-18 war when it was closed, to be opened again in the early 1920s, continuing to operate until its final closure came ten years later. In the 1960s, Dr Beeching's axe fell on the Meon Valley line, bringing about its closure. The line to Winchester closed on Monday 5 February 1973. A sorry sight to see was the last train, a special, leave Alton station on the final run to Winchester on the Sunday evening.

The two latter closures were not understood by the public, as the lines appeared to be kept busy with both passengers and freight. Alton station would be quite busy with passengers waiting to board trains for both routes and there was always considerable activity in the goods yard. During the watercress season, trains on the Meon Valley line brought in consignments of watercress from stations along its length and the containers would be piled on the platform, later to be loaded onto the train up from Winchester, also with its load of cress, to complete its journey to Waterloo.

The closure of the Basingstoke branch line did not really come as a surprise, as most people realised it had been opened for a trial period of about ten years, to see whether it was a viable proposition. But the closure of the other two lines was a different matter.

The haul from Alton to Four Marks, the first station on the Mid-Hants line, was uphill. There was a noticeable difference in the speeds of the trains going up to Four Marks and those coming down to Alton. The goods train made quite a good speed when coming down, but going up the incline when laden was a different matter. This was the day of the 'steamer' and volumes of smoke would be blown out of the locomotive's funnel, as more effort was needed. It was said that going up the first part of the incline the engine would puff: 'Can I do it? Can I do it? Can I do it?', the train reached higher, work became harder and the sound became louder but slower: 'I think I can. I think I can.' But having reached the top of the rise at Four Marks, where the line would be going downhill towards Alresford, the engine would puff quite happily and quickly as it gained speed: 'I knew I could. I knew I could. I knew I could.' One did not need to know anything much about trains to understand what the engine was expressing.

I always felt the Meon Valley line went through some of the most picturesque countryside in the whole country. Cool lush meadows with streams here and there, lovely olde worlde-looking villages nestling among areas of woodland, sometimes with the tower or spire of a church keeping watch over all. Unlike so many train journeys, this one was never boring. It was almost a mini-holiday in itself.

The Mid-Hants line always had the appearance of being the businessman's line. Bowler hats, pinstripes and umbrellas were seen aplenty.

The Basingstoke branch was something of a poor relation, a very relaxed line. Limited to a speed of twenty five miles an hour, one can understand how it was so many people sarcastically referred to the little train as the 'Basingstoke Express'. There were many who, in view of the fact that the train consisted of a small tank engine and a not-too-modern coach, always referred to the train as the 'Sprat and Winkle'.

For all the deriding, it has to be said that it was the Basingstoke branch line which made a greater name for itself. Important visitors, among them on one occasion, the Duke and Duchess of York (later King George VI and Queen Elizabeth the Queen Mother) travelled on special trains from Waterloo to the platform at the Lord Mayor Treloar Cripples' Hospital and College to attend various functions there.

A tank engine also brought trains of coal trucks from Alton goods yard to the hospital siding.

Film makers brought some fame to the line in 1929, when Arnold Ridley's film 'The Wreckers' was made along a stretch of line one Sunday near Herriard. The train crashing into a team wagon loaded with several tons of gravel was a fantastic sight. Gravel and bits of metal from the wagon were thrown over a wide area, and a couple of lengths of rail were removed to complete the derailment and also avoid the risk of the train careering on towards the Butts Junction and Alton station with no crew aboard. The driver had jumped clear after starting the train.

This was not the only time the branch line was used for film-making. There was the time when that very amusing trio, Will Hay, Moore Marriott and Graham Moffat, made the film 'Oh, Mr Porter.'

These days, however, the only sign of the Basingstoke line is a very weedy track through the countryside. Only one of the original lines now remains, the line from Alton to Waterloo. Keen enthusiasts have taken over the station at Alresford and the Mid-Hants track to Alton, which rejoices in the name of 'The Watercress Line'. It cannot reach Winchester as the by-pass at King's Worthy would make any extension in that direction very costly and probably impossible.

7 Hop Picking

I remember how, nearly 70 years ago, we lived in Holybourne, a little village about two miles from the centre of the market town of Alton. There were less than a dozen 'big' houses - and I mean those where the folk occupying them employed maids and a cook to look after running the house for them - and I exclude the three big farmhouses around. The bulk of the dwellings were cottages occupied by a very friendly, kindly lot of villages. In those days there was very little road traffic so it really was a nice quiet rural community.

Somewhere about the end of July and middle of August the village seemed to wake up as thoughts of hop-picking were taking over the minds of the inhabitants. I suppose it was only to be expected, with most of the male wage earners being employed on agricultural or horticultural work which produced poor weekly pay compared with many other jobs, that the chance for the wife and children to earn a little extra was quite important for the family finances.

One began to hear whether the hops were going to be better at Messenger's or Complin's. On the other hand, folk were probably saying that the crop was looking good at Twitchin's up by the church. The talk and speculation continued and ultimately decisions would be made as to which hop garden had the best hops to pick. One farmer, I forget which it was, folk reckoned could be relied on to pay a halfpenny or even a penny (in old money) more per bushel.

Gypsies began to arrive - not the modern travellers with their motor-drawn caravans, but the traditional Romanies with their gaily-coloured caravans pulled by a horse, a cart with children, dogs and goodness knows what loaded into it and perhaps a spare horse tethered at the rear. Beneath some of the vans or carts there was sometimes a sort of built-in hutch with two or three scraggy hens inside; these would be let out to roam around and feed when camp was pitched, but these birds knew their home and would return at night to roost.

The coming of the Romanies meant their womenfolk would be calling on local householders. One of these women would come with a huge carrying basket on one arm displaying oddments of lace, reels of cotton, cards of shirt buttons and so on; another would be selling clothes pegs which the men had made from hazel boughs. It seemed to be characteristic that most of them would offer to tell 'the lady's' fortune. 'Cross your 'and with a bit of silver, lady. You've got a lucky face.'

Public houses all around became busier, leastaways those that did not display the notice 'No Travellers.'

Eventually, the village people would have to come to a decision as to which hop garden they would favour according to reports received on the condition and size of the hops. Families of men working for a farmer growing hops would be expected to 'take a basket' at that farm. Others could be more choosy.

Gypsy families returned to the same farm every year and certain sections of the hop garden would be set aside where they would pick. This was essential as they would sometimes cause trouble, with arguments between themselves and pickers from the village would object to this. It was for this reason that one farmer would only engage local people to pick in his garden.

As newcomers to the village, we knew nothing of these things, but my sister and I, hearing that other children were given a share of their mother's hop-picking earnings, some of which they would spend at the fair held at the end of September in the Market Square in Alton, persuaded mother to go with some village friends who always went hop-picking and 'take a basket' for the three of us.

School holidays were adjusted in the area to cover the 'hopping season' and did not begin until late August and extended through September.

Picking began at eight o'clock in the morning and continued until about five - it had to be a pouring wet day to bring picking to a halt. Each family was issued with a large oval wicker basket reputed to hold seven bushels, with black lines painted around the inside to mark the individual bushels. It was found, however, hops being crushable, after one achieved the five bushel mark, more than another actual bushel would be needed to bring the contents up to the six bushel line. The added weight of the additional hops compressed those below and caused them to sink.

Each basket holder was allocated an 'alley' or row of hops. The hop bines (in some areas these are referred to as hop vines but locally they were always called bines) climbed up strings to the wire which ran along the tops of a line of posts some nine or ten feet high. Thus, the alley was something of a tunnel roofed with green leaves and hops. Often the string up which the bine had climbed was weathered enough to break away from the top wire when pulled, but this was not always the case. There was always a man in the garden, armed with a long pole with a blade at one end, with which he would cut the string, allowing the bine to fall across the basket. This man was still called the 'pole puller', although there were very few hop gardens at that time still using poles, up which the hops were trained.

I am sure autumn and winter in those days were very much colder than they are today, as many of those September days began with frosty mornings. One year, we were picking at Messenger's farm at Bonhams. To reach the farm, we took a short cut across a field by the blacksmiths where there was a very large horse chestnut tree, then across a lane to a field which I think was called Butcher's Meadow. The grass was all white with hoar frost and puddles in the lane covered with ice. In this field, the gypsies who were picking in Messenger's hop garden were allowed to camp and their caravans, carts and tents were around the edges. Horses were staked out, lurcher dogs were hunting around for any edible scraps and the hens were doing the same. Wood smoke from the many fires, over which stood or hung from tripods the pots and kettles, lay heavily on the frosty air. The gypsies appeared happy enough and called out 'Good morning' to anyone passing. Washing was hanging from a few lines and some was also draped over a handy bush here and there.

On these frosty mornings, it was not at all pleasant until the sun came up well off the horizon and gathered some strength to warm up the atmosphere. In spite of the fact that most folk wore some old gloves or mittens, their fingers still became so cold it was necessary to stop picking and do something about rubbing feeling back into their hands. Children sat on stools or boxes picking from a bine which had been pulled down for them. They used a box, old basket or perhaps a tin bath for the purpose and, when the receptacles were full, emptied them into a very large sack (called a surplice). Until the air warmed and thawed the frost sufficiently, every time a bine was pulled or even shaken, a shower of ice droplets fell onto all the pickers in the alley from the hops and leaves; later, when the ice thawed it was water which showered down upon us.

Local schoolmasters usually undertook the job of tallying ie. measuring the quantity of hops in our baskets and recording the number of bushels each of us had picked against each basket-holder's number in their log books. Tallying usually took place about midday and again when the pole puller blew his whistle at about five o'clock to signify that picking for the day had finished. We took each big basket to the end of the alley for the tally to be taken. Afterwards, two men up-ended each basket's contents into a surplice which, when full, was tied up and heaved onto a horse-drawn cart for transportation to the hop kiln for drying.

The rate of pay for each bushel varied from threepence halfpenny to ninepence (the latter would be a very good price, paid to those who picked smaller, poor quality hops; if this higher price was not paid, nobody would pick them). As I recall, the rate generally received was about sixpence a bushel - up or down a halfpenny or so. The picking period might last up to a maximum of maybe three weeks and a good day's picking could result in a total of twelve or fourteen bushels. I cannot be sure of this, but mother's payment may have been eight or nine pounds - some people might have received more and others less. We knew the gypsies earned more because of the number of people they had picking at each basket. Some people also received more because they snatched the hops off with a considerable number of leaves which they did not remove from the basket.

After mother received payment for all our labours, she gave me and my sister a small amount to spend at the fair and something to save. She would probably also buy an article of clothing for us.

One Sunday towards the end of hop-picking, at Bentley, just inside the Surrey border about halfway between Holybourne and Farnham, the gypsies used to hold their fair. This was not an amusement fair like the one held in Alton's Market Square, but one where they bought, sold and exchanged horses, carts and tack. It was a very busy scene with horses and carts being raced along the road in demonstration.

The last time I was in that area some years ago, I saw no hop gardens and was given to understand very few now remained in the Alton district.

Alas, another link with Hampshire's past has gone.

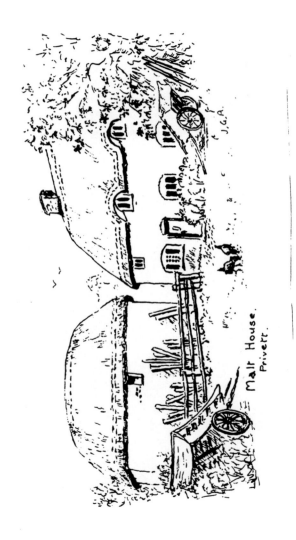

8 The Old Malt House at Privett

The March day had been extremely cold with a bitter north-easterly wind blowing, with occasional flakes of snow. My wife-to-be Win and I were visiting her granny at the old 'Malt House' at Privett. My 1928 Austin Seven 'Chummy' tourer, which only had celluloid-type side screens and no heater, did nothing to counteract the almost arctic temperature outside.

The big gate which gave access to the forecourt of the dwelling was always open to admit passing carts and wagons into the yard for repairs. To one side was the big thatched barn and there were two farm carts waiting for repairs to be carried out to the bodies, or new wheels to be made and fitted. A little way off was the sawpit which allowed two of my fiancée's uncles to use a cross-cut saw to cut the timbers they needed for their work. One would be above ground and the other in the pit below. The Ayling family were highly thought of in the neighbourhood. They had carried on the business of wheelrights, estate carpenters and undertakers here for something like two hundred years. This fine old house had not been new even then, when the early members of the family first moved in.

Beyond the cobblestone areas was the old thatched house itself, mellowed by the centuries. With its thick thatched roof and 'eyebrows' over the bedroom windows, the whole place emanated an air of charm, calm and comfort; three 'Cs' which mean so much in this hectic life of ours today. The same feeling was there at the time of which I now write, more than fifty years ago.

The building looked solid. The windows, unlike the large picture windows of today, were small but quite adequate and gave one the feeling the inhabitants had so much more privacy, with the ability to look out on the world without the world being able to look in at them.

At the door, one noticed the stone step, probably the same one laid there when the house was built. It had been worn down by the passing of so many feet throughout the decades that, had a square-edge been laid on the stone it would have shown well over an inch had been eroded in the centre over the years.

It was good to arrive indoors and shut out the elements which still tried to win by blowing a fierce draught below the outer door. This could only be combated by a piece of matting along the bottom of the door.

The warm air was most welcome. Our cold red noses picked up the homely farmhouse smell of stored apples, wood smoke and probably some animal feed stored somewhere in the house. This reminded me of the smell in a corn chandler's. These smells, and the general comfortable atmosphere of the place, gave it the air of good honest living. There was talking when we entered, of course, as three uncles and two aunts were there with Granny Ayling, though all but granny and uncle Alf were on their way to evensong at Privett church. The church, alas, when I last saw it was unused, with doors barred and windows boarded up. From uncle Will's terraced corrage nearby, ivy was twining its way in and out of the bedroom window, a reminder both he and aunt Edie had been dead for many years.

One came to understand why in days gone by it was sensible to have three-legged stools. Three-legged seats were the only items which would stand firmly without rocking on worn and uneven brick floors. The floor in this very big kitchen was certainly uneven. I must say, though, the heavy six or eight foot long deal kitchen table showed no sign of rocking. But I never inspected it to see whether one of the legs had been fitted with a chock to keep it steady.

The ceiling, of course, was lower than present-day ceilings. The heavy oak open beams were mellowed in keeping with everything around and gave the feeling of great solidity. Oil lamps and candles were the only means of illumination, apart that is, from the great flames leaping up from the huge log fire burning on the hearth in the inglenook fireplace. The stone hearth was raised an inch or two above the level of the brick floor, and at each side of the fire in the chimney recess was a bench large enough to accommodate two persons on each. Here one was away from the draughts of the room, about which great displays of light danced on the ceilings and walls as the flames from the burning logs flew up into the wide mouth of the chimney, up which sides of bacon could be smoke-cured.

Though one was in the recess beside the fire and away from any draughts in the room, I must admit the March wind did succeed in finding a way in, down the chimney from time to time. This was probably how the clinging wood smoke permeated the atmosphere of the house. It certainly did penetrate the clothes one was wearing. Although I did not find this particularly unpleasant, I didn't appreciate the odd soot smut adhering to my clothes. When the weather was calm and frosty there was no downdraught. Without the smoke and smuts being blown over one, sitting at the side of the huge fire was very pleasant indeed.

Now, fifty years on, granny Ayling and all the uncles and aunts have left this earth. Most unfortunately, so has Win, the girl who used to take me to the old Malt House and who later became my wife. On my visit to the village two or three years ago, after the lapse of many years, I found the house had not been even as fortunate as the church was. At least the church was still standing. There was no sign of the Malt House which I had once known. The house, together with the old thatched barn, had been demolished and a modern dwelling built on the site, which just carried the name Malt House Farm, a reminder to me of what had once been a wonderful old-world thatched home with a lovely family living in it.

9 The School at Lane End

The A272 road from Winchester to Petersfield passes through some delightful Hampshire countryside. It passes through, or by, several charming villages: Cheriton, Hinton Ampner and Bramdean, to mention but three. From Winchester, the road makes a long ascent to pass over Cheesefoot Head, known to many local people as Chesford Head. From the highest point, the road runs down until one comes to a turning on the right-hand side by Warren Farm. This branch continues right through to the village of Warnford on the Meon Valley road.

Shortly after leaving the A272, this very narrow secondary road crosses another, leading to Longwood, Owslebury and Marwell, ultimately joining the Winchester/Bishop's Waltham road. However, by continuing in the direction of Warnford, the road descends beside what was known as Lane End Down. This area used to be unfenced downland where harebells and delicate shiver-grass flourished, but it is now fenced and under cultivation since decreed by the Hampshire Agricultural Committee early in the Second World War.

At the bottom of the downland, one reaches Lane End, where a narrow lane runs off to the right to Lane End Farm and then on out into the countryside. Lane End is not a village, nor even a hamlet. The two tiled cottages on the corner of the lane were not built until the latter half of the nineteenth century. The land around belongs to the Longwood Estate and at the time the owner, Earl Northesk, was living at Longwood Mansion House. It was he who had these two cottages built and an engraved stone on them bears the letters 'W.H.E.N.' standing for William Hopetoun, Earl of Northesk.

In 1875, the knapped flint building of the school, incorporating the schoolhouse, was erected and opened in 1876 to replace the little school which had existed at Beauworth. It was said the flints, or many of them, were picked up by mothers of those children who had to walk cross-country to school. In those days, parents had to pay for their children's education and supposedly the stone-picking was to help with this. Lane End school was also used for church services as an adjunct to Cheriton Church and the vicar used to travel from there to Lane End by pony and trap. Children were also baptised in the school, using a toilet basin as a font.

The land on which the school was built was given by Lord Northesk and, what is rather odd, according to old farm records the name of the field of which the school land was part, was known as 'Knowledge's'. One assumes Knowledge was the name of a previous farmer who used the field. It would appear this seat of learning was truly based on the field of knowledge.

In 1904, a little way up from the school, two houses were built to be the retirement homes of Walter and Ann Brown and William and Caroline Tithecott. The two latter had been living at Hamilton Farm, Beauworth and William was cabinet maker to Early Northesk. In those days, most of the large pieces of furniture were made on site to fit the house. My grandfather held a similar position many years earlier, for the Northesk family at Marwell Hall.

Just down the lane from the school stood the blacksmith's and farrier's forge belonging to Walter Brown. His wife Ann was first headmistress of the school. They had a son and a daughter, Daniel and Millicent. Daniel married Ethel Ayling from Privett who became the last headmistress of Lane End school. Caroline Tithecott, 'Ki' to all the family, was a teacher at the school for a number of years.

I first met the Browns and Tithecotts at the time my family went to visit them when I was a boy of 14. Daniel Brown and his wife, then in charge of the school, were living in the schoolhouse with their two children Winifred and Walter. Winifred was six but on the next occasion I took my mother to visit Lane End, she was 16. From then, I visited Lane End regularly. By then, the family had moved to the cottages up the lane. Winifred and I married five years later and enjoyed a very happy married life until she was taken ill suddenly and died in 1979.

I recall ex-pupils calling to see their former teachers, long after the school closed. Mrs Tithecott, only five feet in height, was overshadowed by many of them. I recall one Boxing Day evening we were sat by a roaring fire in the little parlour at Mrs Tithecott's house when ten people arrived, two former pupils with their wives and families, to give their former teacher seasonal greetings. Mrs Tithecott was 80-plus, but she still was the school marm of old. She stamped her tiny foot on the floor once and, with a low but commanding voice, uttered just one word, 'Silence.' A hush fell on the room immediately and this enabled teacher to say her piece.

Sadly, in 1922, the authorities closed the school. It took about a year to persuade the children to go to the new school at the Millbarrows, pronounced Millberries by local people.

Mrs Ethel Brown died in 1935, but Mrs Tithecott lived on for a number of years, dying at 90 in a hospital bed in Winchester, still under the impression the nursing staff were children in one of her classes.

Lane End is not the centre it was for generations of children. The blacksmith's forge and William Tithecott's workshop opposite it have disappeared. The school has been a private residence for many years. Nothing can detract from the benefits and good which resulted from the contact of those devoted teachers with the children under their care and influence in this little Hampshire school.

The school building, like so many other such, will no doubt stand for many years. There must have been much satisfaction to teachers and parents in having these country schools, most of which were of elegant appearance. With their passing, perhaps one could use as a fitting epitaph '*Sic transit gloria mundi.*'

10 Deflation at the Treloar Hospital

The Lord Mayor Treloar Hospital in Alton is now in use again after several years standing empty. The Treloar Hospital and College, Alton, was begun by Sir William Purdie Treloar solely for the treatment of children with physical disabilities. About 50 older boys, also disabled, were catered for at the college, where they learnt leatherwork, bag making, boot making and tailoring, to equip them to earn a living as independent craft workers when they left. The hospital in Alton catered for about 340 children suffering from tubercular diseases. Later, at Sandy Point, Hayling Island, another smaller unit for about 50 children was started for the benefit of children at Alton who were being rested from treatment and given the benefit of sea and air. At Alton, upwards of 300 children - from infants to 16 year-olds - were accommodated at the time of which I write, in the timber-built wards arranged in two semi-circular blocks.

I was employed as inventory clerk at the hospital from 1928 to 1933. At that time the college and hospital workshops were accommodated in timber buildings. I believe the hospital was built originally under a scheme known as 'The Absent-Minded Beggars' Fund', catering for wounded soldiers returning from the South African war.

In hospital, there is always pain and suffering, but there is also happiness and in this children's hospital amusing things often happened. The head clerk, Mr. Arthur Exton, owned a sparkling B.S.A. motor cycle which stood out at the hospital, because nobody else owned one. A few senior staff had cars.

After visiting his father some weekends in Southsea, Arthur would return straight to the hospital on Monday and would park the cycle outside the office, next to a pillar box. Just below the office was a ward of about 20 boys aged eight to ten. When their lessons finished, they would gather round the motor cycle in admiration. Arthur would go out and answer their questions with great pleasure. One of these boys was little Johnny Baldwin.

I don't whether Arthur wished to raise his status at work. Whatever the reason, he bought a Jowett two-seater tourer with a dickey seat, from Barnett and Small of Farnham. It was a rather stunted looking car, second- or maybe third-hand, with a twin-cylinder engine sounding as though it was suffering and wondering whether to carry on functioning or give up the ghost.

Well, Arthur cleaned and polished his car and in due course it appeared in front of the office one Monday morning. Some members of staff came and spoke to Arthur about the car and he went out with them to allow them to inspect it. I could see he took quite a pride in this.

Lunchtime came. Out went Arthur wearing the large gauntlets he'd used for motor cycling and which he now used for driving his tourer. Two or three little boys were looking quizzically round the car. They turned and saw him and it was Johnny Baldwin who spoke:

'Is this yours Mr Exton?'

'Yes, Johnny, it's mine,' Arthur answered with much conviction.

'Where's your motor bike then?'

'It's gone Johnny, sold.'

'Cor, and you say this is yours.?'

'Yes, that's right.'

Johnny paused, walked along to the side of the car, noting it had obviously seen a good deal of use and, with the single-minded directness of a child, added,

'Well, where did you get it Mr Exton? Did you win it in a raffle?'

I doubt whether that little boy ever deflated anyone so much in later life as he deflated Arthur Exton in that moment.

Autumn Fruits.

11 Christmas at Treloars

Over 60 years ago, in my work in the Steward's department at the Treloar Hospital in Alton and I noticed how every year as Christmas approach the youngsters' excitement built up. For all these young patients, as with children everywhere, Christmas was a very special time of year, perhaps more especially for those whose treatment and stay in hospital had been extended to several years. In the College section were 50 disabled boys coming into their late teens who were under training in a trade they hoped ultimately to pursue. Most of these boys went home for Christmas.

Normally, there were discharges from the hospital every two weeks, of those children whose treatment had been completed. There was always much envy of those going home, especially for those going home for Christmas, by the patients who were staying. A number of the children came from very poor areas, some even from the workhouses of those days, so they were not all returning to comfortable homes and loving families. In some cases, children would have a better time staying in the hospital.

Several days before Christmas was over, Gaumont British News came to the hospital to make a film showing what would happen on Christmas morning. Waiting for the filming to begin was the medical superintendent, Sir Henry Gauvain, ready dressed for the part of Santa Claus, with a sack of presents.

The hospital's two assistant medical officers were Santa's helpers, Dr. E. M. Jones, a well-built man of over six feet in height, who was amusingly dressed as a fairy with a tinsel and white short ballet dress, white socks, carrying a wand. The second doctor was dressed in the costume of a cat.

Unfortunately, especially for Dr. Jones in his scanty fairy attire, the morning was cold and frosty. The film crew were very late arriving and the person who was suffering most, standing outside on the solarium which was to be the first set, was the fairy, Dr Jones. He was an inveterate pipe-smoker and I must say he looked most droll, puffing away at his pipe and dressed as he was. I shall not repeat the comments made by him as he stamped around in the cold, as they were not at all fairylike.

Years roll by. The doctors who took part in that film ended their earthly medical duties many years ago and any of the children who were in the hospital then and are still alive could be grandparents. But there is no doubt, one could truthfully say at Treloar's a Merry Christmas indeed was had by all.

oOOOo

Passing Time

The months, the days, so quickly go,
Taking the friends I used to know.
The places which I used to see
No longer now remain to me.

Old friends again I'd love to see.
I wonder would they now know me.
The only time we meet it seems
Is when I see them in my dreams.

The carrier with his horse and van
Has long since gone, and where he ran
Buses now pass along the road.
Of course, they take a bigger load.

Shops are bigger and houses too,
Changed are all those things we knew.
Colonies in high flats dwell -
A life that would not suit me well.

We may not like things as they are
And to our eyes a lot may jar,
To have lived when I did, I'm sure
Rejoices me - I am not sore.

The Author's Wife 'Win' at 'Clovelly', Lane End, around 1930.